A 30 Day Devotional for Mothers

Challenges *in the* Joy *of* Motherhood

Prayers From a Mother's Heart

by
Charity L. Lloyd

McDougal Publishing is a ministry of The McDougal Foundation, Inc., a Maryland
nonprofit corporation dedicated to spreading the Gospel of the Lord Jesus Christ
to as many people as possible in the shortest time possible.

Published by:
McDougal Publishing
P.O. Box 3595
Hagerstown, MD 21742-3595
www.mcdougalpublishing.com

ISBN 1-58158-102-5

Printed in the United States of America
For Worldwide Distribution

Dedication

To my Lord and Savior Jesus Christ,
who keeps me on the potter's wheel

To my husband,
who loves me unconditionally

To my family and friends,
who constantly encourage me

And especially to my children,
who teach me the joy of mothering

Loving Them

You have just spent nine months of your life preparing for that precious little bundle. The physical changes in your body and the pain which brought forth your child were the easy part. Now comes the hard part, raising them. Child rearing is one of the hardest tasks any one person will attempt in life. But do not despair. There is hope. His name is Jesus Christ.

Raising godly children is not only possible but also attainable in this day.

Jesus looked at them and said to them, "With men this is impossible, but with God all things are possible."
Matthew 19:26, NKJ

The new commandment Jesus gave to us was to love one another as He has loved us. This includes those little people in our lives that we claim as our children.

Love suffers long and is kind; love does not envy; love does not parade itself, is not puffed up; does not behave rudely, does not seek its own, is not provoked, thinks no evil; does not

rejoice in iniquity, but rejoices in the truth; bears all things,
believes all things, hopes all things, endures all things.
                              1 Corinthians 13:4-7, NKJ

I had to ask myself some questions. Do I love my children? Am I committed to them? What am I doing and why am I doing it? It is the same as asking, Do I love You, Lord? Am I committed to You?

Are we babysitting our children or are we training our children? Do we allow our children to see Christ working in our lives? Are we going through the motions while the day when they will be adults draws near? We could be mentoring a present-day Elijah or Esther and not even realize it.

We will stand accountable for our children and for how we brought them up. Therefore, we must not entertain thoughts of putting the responsibility on day cares, schools, or even our churches.

Therefore, my beloved brethren, be steadfast, immovable, always
abounding in the work of the Lord, knowing that your labor
is not in vain in the Lord. [The labors of love that we
endure as parents will not be in vain.]
                              1 Corinthians 15:58, NKJ

We must take time to listen to our children. If we are not interested in and active in the lives of our children, they will turn to someone who will be. When we finally make time for them, they may not be interested in spending time with us. In these last days, we must not be conformed to this world but rather be transformed by Jesus Christ. Children will learn what they see. Our actions sometimes speak louder than our words.

Contents

Day 1 - Rest

Dear Lord,

I am so tired. It seems as though all I have done lately is take care of everyone else's needs except my own. Most days I can hardly find time to be in Your Word, and I long to have fellowship with You. Today I want to be able to lay my head on my pillow in sweet peace. I am pulled in so many different directions, and everyone wants my attention. I know that in You there is rest. Help me to find it. This time of my life while my children are young is so hard sometimes. I know that You understand. Strengthen my body and multiply the amount of sleep I get so that it feels like more. Help me to get through one more day. Teach me to depend on You for my rest so that I can pass this trait on to my children. As they see me casting my cares and burdens upon You, I believe that they will learn to do the same. Help me to use my time wisely and to take advantage of little naps throughout the day. Help me to keep my priorities in order so that I make good use of my time. Help me not to use the nighttime hours to catch up on daily chores that are not so important. My sleep right now is vital for me to be effective as a mother. Keep me in Your perfect rest.

Amen.

A Mother's Prayer for Rest:

_____

_____

_____

_____

_____

_____

_____

_____

_____

_____

_____

_____

_____

Amen.

"Come to me, all you who are weary and burdened, and I will give you rest."   Matthew 11:28 NIV

Day 2 - Pain

Dear Lord,

My children hurt me today by their words and actions and I feel so unappreciated and taken for granted. I need Your help to get past this. Use me to turn the other cheek in fairness and not to react to my flesh and that desire to hurt in return. I am the adult in this situation, I know. Yet I hurt too. Teach me how I should train my children so that they are aware of the feelings of those around them. Let me show them how their behavior may hurt others. I know there will be times when they also will experience hurt and pain. Use these hard times in our lives not to tear us down, but as opportunities to learn to do unto others as we would have them do unto us. Help me to build my children's character and affirm them in such a way that they would not feel the need to intentionally hurt. I can find comfort in You through my pain. Help me to model and build a loving spirit within my children. Your Word is so prominent in my life and I want to share this with them. I know, Lord that You have experienced both physical and emotional hurt. I also know that through this pain You will use me to minister to others in need. Sometimes it hurts to grow. Use every opportunity in my life, whether the hurt is physical or emotional, to glorify You and to continue to build character in my children.

Amen.

A Mother's Prayer for Pain:

_____

_____

_____

_____

_____

_____

_____

_____

_____

_____

_____

_____

_____

_____

_____

Amen.

The righteous face many troubles, but the LORD rescues them from each and every one. Psalm 34:19

Day 3 - Leadership

Dear Lord,

One of my heart's desires is not necessarily to have my children grow up and become president of the United States or CEO of a major corporation. If that is Your will for them, then I encourage it. I know that the best leaders are ones who recognize their need of a savior and their need of help from others. I pray that they would demonstrate leadership in every area of their lives. Help them not to just sit back and be idle, but to take the initiative and be leaders even if it means they stand alone. May they know and trust that You are always with them. Help them to know through my life that effective leadership starts with serving others as unto the Lord and not unto men. A wise leader can change the direction of an entire army. Let them take their leadership responsibility seriously, and please show me early on the plans that You have for their lives and how I can have a positive effect on them. Help me to lead and direct them in the purposes You have for each one of them.

Amen.

A Mother's Prayer for Leadership:

_____

_____

_____

_____

_____

_____

_____

_____

_____

_____

_____

_____

_____

_____

_____

Amen.

If God has given you leadership ability, take the responsibility
seriously.   Romans 12:8

Day 4 - Friendship

Dear Lord,

My children will have many friendships throughout their lives. I pray that they will all be good and uplifting relationships. Many people will cross their paths, and them as well. I know that in order to find and keep friends, we must show ourselves friendly. Lord, help me to be a good friend to the people in my life, and allow my children to see this. I pray that they would make friends easily and never allow the enemy to make them feel alone. Help my children to choose their friendships wisely as I try to do also. Instill in them the sensitivity that will warn them of unhealthy relationships. Help them not to be pulled by peer pressure into the kind of relationships the world has to offer. Let these things not look good to them. While they are still small, I have much control over their friendships. I know that as they grow, challenges will arise. I ask You to help me to guard their hearts and minds and not allow any friendships to come between my children and me. More importantly, let them value their relationship with You. Let them know that You are the best friend they could ever have.

Amen.

A Mother's Prayer for Friendship:

_____

_____

_____

_____

_____

_____

_____

_____

_____

_____

_____

_____

_____

_____

_____

Amen.

There are "friends" who destroy each other, but a real friend sticks closer than a brother.   Proverbs 18:24

Day 5 - Protection

Dear Lord,

The very first time I let my children sleep away from home I wanted to go bring them back half a dozen times. Lord, it is so hard to let go. I know I must give You complete control for them to mature not only physically but, more importantly, spiritually. I know that I can trust You for their safety. Just as You protected Your Son Jesus through all that He endured, I know You will protect my children too. I know I can trust You completely for their care and protection. I know that You have angels encamped around them to guard them and that You will not allow them to dash their foot against a stone. At the same time, I also know that You will use circumstances in their lives that are necessary but may sometimes be painful. They will need You to shape and mold them into the persons that You have ordained for them to be. Just as Mary pondered so many things in her heart, I know that this will be a hard time and an adjustment period for me. Help me to get through this and to encourage them to place their trust in You, seeing that I do it first. Just knowing how You care about the sparrow makes letting go so much easier for me. I know that Your love and protection are beyond what I can understand or imagine.

Amen.

A Mother's Prayer for Protection:

_____

_____

_____

_____

_____

_____

_____

_____

_____

_____

_____

_____

_____

_____

_____

Amen.

For he orders his angels to protect you wherever you go.
Psalm 91:11

Day 6 - Words

Dear Lord,

The tongue is such a small member of the body, yet it can cause great damage. Help me to teach my children the power of their words at a young age. Help them to always choose to encourage and affirm others rather than to tear down and condemn. When we are hurt, it is so easy to want to retaliate with our mouths. Help me to have self-control and use my words wisely and lovingly. Allow my children to see specific instances in which I choose words of life versus words of death. Let my children be known, esteemed, and trusted by their words. I pray that they would not add or take away but let their yes be yes and their no be no. Also, let me not be tempted to change my words when I have given my yes or no. Help me not to feel pressured to go against my word. I know that if I constantly do this, my word will mean nothing to them. Help them to follow through with the verbal commitments that they make. Let them always honor and glorify You with their lips. I know that sometimes the more we say, the less people will listen to us. Help my children not to be like sounding brass or a clanging cymbal.

Amen.

A Mother's Prayer for Words:

_____

_____

_____

_____

_____

_____

_____

_____

_____

_____

_____

_____

_____

_____

_____

Amen.

Above all, my brothers, do not swear—not by heaven or by earth or by anything else. Let your "Yes" be yes, and your "No," no, or you will be condemned. James 5:12

Day 7 - Gossip

Dear Lord,

I overheard one of my children retelling a story that someone had told him. It was something that should not have been repeated. I am aware of the havoc that gossip can cause in the lives of real people. I have seen it separate friends and betray confidences. Gossip is no respecter of persons and will destroy anyone in its path. It has shattered lives and wrecked relationships. Help me to teach my children even at this young age that gossip is wrong. Develop in me ways to convey this to them at their level of understanding. As they grow, because we have dealt with this at an early age, gossip will not be a part of their lives. It is not "sharing", as some may consider it to be. Let there be no gray areas for gossip in my children's lives and in my life as well. Start first with me. I know that what I do and with whom I speak and what conversations I hold will speak louder than any lesson that I may try to teach my children. Convict me, Lord, if I fail in this area, and strengthen me to admit my weaknesses. Let gossip not be a part of my life. If I would begin to gossip or speak in a way that doesn't glorify You and Your holy name, please quickly bring it to my attention. Work in me and perfect these things that concern my children, and then enable me to do Your will in their lives.

Amen.

A Mother's Prayer for Gossip:

_____
_____
_____
_____
_____
_____
_____
_____
_____
_____
_____
_____
_____
_____
_____
_____

Amen.

A troublemaker plants seeds of strife; gossip separates the best of friends. Proverbs 16:28

Day 8 - Purity

Dear Lord,

I want physical and spiritual purity in the lives of my children. Adolescence can be very demanding and burdening for young people. For some, a lot of decisions and choices made during this time can affect them into adulthood. Lord, please keep my children pure. Not only in their walk with You, but pure in their bodies also. Let them remain virgins until marriage and set a new standard for others around them. I know that we are pure because of You. The sin we once carried, as red as crimson, You washed as white as snow. I want my children to remain pure, not only to keep their bodies as a gift to You, but also not to allow temptations of the mind to overcome them. I pray that the mistakes I made will never be mistakes that my children will make. The ways that I did not trust in You and allowed my spirit, soul, mind and body, to become impure will not be a path my children will ever take. Let their virginity be a gift not only to You but also to their mates. I also ask You to provide mates for them who also have remained pure. I will not believe that this is impossible even in this day we are living in. I know that as they keep their minds steadfast on You, when the temptation to be impure arises, they will use Your Word and what I have taught them through Your grace. In Your holy name, I pray that every temptation that arises in their lives, through Your strength they will overcome and not fall into it.

Amen.

A Mother's Prayer for Purity:

_____

_____

_____

_____

_____

_____

_____

_____

_____

_____

_____

_____

_____

_____

_____

Amen.

How can a young person stay pure? By obeying your word and following its rules. Psalm 119:9

Day 9 - Laziness

Dear Lord,

It is so easy to be lazy in this cyber world we live in. Everything, with a click of a mouse, is right at our fingertips for our discretion. Even though these things may be good, they may not be good for us. Help me to instill in my children that there is no greater feeling of satisfaction than there is in a hard day's work, knowing that you truly did your best at something and didn't try to take a shortcut along the way, that you worked at something with your whole heart. Many people may try to teach that getting something for nothing is the smart way to live. It wasn't smart in the past, nor is it smart today. Help me to go that extra mile. Whenever we head out to the grocery store, we see grocery carts all over the parking lot, anywhere except where they belong. I can talk about not being lazy all I want, but if I cannot even take my grocery cart to the proper place, it will go in one of my children's ears and out the other. Help me to use and teach the thirty-second rule to my children. If it can be done in thirty seconds, do it. It is not healthy for my children to be lazy. Let them see, through my example, that physically their bodies need to be mobile and to get the proper amount of exercise. I pray that they would serve others and not only themselves. Help them to be the first to help pick up something that is dropped. Continue to use me and keep me on my toes so that I would never give them an example of laziness.

Amen.

A Mother's Prayer for Laziness:

_____

_____

_____

_____

_____

_____

_____

_____

_____

_____

_____

_____

_____

_____

_____

Amen.

A little extra sleep, a little more slumber, a little folding of the hands to rest—and poverty will pounce on you like a bandit; scarcity will attack you like an armed robber.

Proverbs 6:10-11

Day 10 - Compassion

Dear Lord,

I pray that a commercial depicting starving people would never come across our TV screen and we would be so hard-hearted that we feel nothing or that it doesn't move us. I know that when something happens repeatedly, sometimes our hearts grow cold toward it. Help my children never to lose compassion for people and circumstances. I pray that their hearts would always remain fertile ground and soft. Lord, You had so much compassion that You sent Your one and only Son to save a lost and dying world. There have been times when I have had no regard for life. Help me to realize that even stepping on an ant on purpose could make a lasting impression on my children. I am not saying that we have to tiptoe through this world, just be mindful of our surroundings. Jesus had so much compassion for the sick and anyone else in need. As their mother, my children will watch everything I do. Help me also not to lose compassion for my children. Some days are hard and my heart feels hard toward them. Help me to keep in touch with You at all times. Help me to always hear Your voice. I pray You would continue to have compassion for my children and never stop teaching me to have compassion for others.

Amen.

A Mother's Prayer for Compassion:

_____

_____

_____

_____

_____

_____

_____

_____

_____

_____

_____

_____

_____

_____

_____

Amen.

Have mercy on me, O God, because of your unfailing love. Because of your great compassion, blot out the stain of my sins. Psalm 51:1

Day 11 - Honesty

Dear Lord,

It is so important to be truthful. Help me, Lord, to recognize that even a small white lie breaks Your law. Help me to teach my children that honesty is still the best policy. I do not want my children to be labeled as persons who lie. I know that even one lie can tarnish their character. Even the lie that is never known by man will always be known by You, Lord. I know that You hate dishonesty. Help me to strive for honesty in my life in all circumstances. I pray that when my children become adults, they will continue to be honest not only in the things that You call them to do but also in their daily life activities. I pray that they would not lie for their own gain. I pray that as they climb the ladder of life, it would not be at whatever the cost. Continue to work through me so I can continue to work what is true and important. Let my children be fair to all those around them. Let them remain true, honest, and just in all their ways and, above all, pleasing in Your sight.

Amen.

A Mother's Prayer for Honesty:

_____

_____

_____

_____

_____

_____

_____

_____

_____

_____

_____

_____

_____

_____

Amen.

I will be careful to live a blameless life—when will you come to my aid? I will lead a life of integrity in my own home. I will refuse to look at anything vile and vulgar. I hate all crooked dealings; I will have nothing to do with them.

Psalm 101:2-3

Day 12 - Fear

Dear Lord,

With God on my side, what can man do to me? This scripture is comforting. Your Word promises that You will never leave or forsake us. Yet fear still grips my heart. At times my children also are afraid. It may be because of a circumstance, a person, a test at school, even the dark sometimes. Teach me to comfort them. Remind me that You are always with us. When it is dark, remind me that Your light within me will shine through and light the way. Even the smallest amount of light dispels darkness. When You allow circumstances into my life that make me feel alone, use them to allow my children to see me reaching out to You and You reaching back to comfort me. Although things in this life may make them feel scared, equip me to show them through Your Word that You are full of light and that You will light our path. You have promised to guide and direct our lives; help me as I instill this promise in them.

Amen.

A Mother's Prayer for Fear:

_____

_____

_____

_____

_____

_____

_____

_____

_____

_____

_____

_____

_____

_____

_____

Amen.

That is why we can say with confidence, "The Lord is my helper, so I will not be afraid. What can mere mortals do to me?"   Hebrews 13:6

Day 13 - Seasons

Dear Lord,

Why does it seem like winter will never end? At times I get so caught up in one particular season with my children that I forget that there are other seasons. It seems I get caught up in winter more often than I'd like. I know my children sense this in my life. I also know that You will use this to allow them to see that I am a real person, that I am someone who has feelings and who does not do all things perfectly. I am someone who makes mistakes and suffers consequences. In winter, everything around me seems dead. There is no visible life. It is cold and dark. Let me not forget that although there is no visible life, there is life in the ground at the roots. Nature is resting and rejuvenating itself. Let me use winter to rest and rejuvenate as well. When my children go through winter in their lives, teach me to show them that as we wait patiently on You, we can trust that You are sending spring our way. Allow the winter to be a time of growth in my life and in the lives of my children even when we cannot see it.

Amen.

A Mother's Prayer for Seasons:

_____

_____

_____

_____

_____

_____

_____

_____

_____

_____

_____

_____

_____

_____

Amen.

Be still in the presence of the LORD, and wait patiently for him to act.　　　　　　　　　　　Psalm 37:7

Day 14 - Confidence

Dear Lord,

I want my children to display godly confidence, not worldly confidence, in their lives. Just as Paul could have boasted of himself, instead he chose to boast of the ways of the Lord. I pray my children would continually put their trust and confidence in You and not in any other person, not even me. I know that I can fail them at times, but that You will never fail them. I want them to trust You and Your ways and not their own ways. Our ways often lead to trouble and sometimes to spiritual death. I pray that they would have confidence that You will not only hear their prayers but answer them too. I want them to be confident in their salvation through You. I know that as they grow they will grasp Your saving power by grace and they will walk confidently in that knowledge. Help them not to be ignorant of the ways of this world but to be aware of their surroundings. I pray that they would never be overcome by their circumstances. Bless them as they continue to strive for excellence by putting their complete confidence in You. May they always have God confidence.

Amen.

A Mother's Prayer for Confidence:

_____

_____

_____

_____

_____

_____

_____

_____

_____

_____

_____

_____

_____

_____

_____

                                          Amen.

*"Blessed are those who trust in the LORD and have made the
LORD their hope and confidence. They are like trees planted
along a riverbank, with roots that reach deep into the water."*
                                          Jeremiah 17:7-8a

Day 15 - Contentment

Dear Lord,

Help me to be content in all of the circumstances that come into my life. How many times I catch myself comparing myself with other people. Comparing what You have given to me with the blessings You have given to others. I know that this is a setup to cause me to grumble, complain, and enter into self-pity. I know that the enemy would like to keep me in a state of discontentment. This is a characteristic I would never want to pass on to my children. I pray that they would find true contentment through You. I ask that they would not be complacent either. Please allow them to always be teachable and ready to hear a word from You. Help me to learn in whatever situation You allow me to be in that I can be content, and provide me teaching opportunities for my children. Help me not to compare my children with other children and thus allow a root of discontentment to begin to grow. Help me to teach my children that money and materialism will provide only temporary contentment. Teach them through my life that only through Jesus can there be everlasting contentment. For young children, the average time spent with the newest toy is about five minutes. As they grow and mature, let the joy of contentment through You be more appealing than any worldly thing. Let it be evident to them that true contentment through You leads to abundant life.

Amen.

A Mother's Prayer for Contentment:

_____

_____

_____

_____

_____

_____

_____

_____

_____

_____

_____

_____

_____

_____

Amen.

We didn't bring anything with us when we came into the world, and we certainly cannot carry anything with us when we die. So if we have enough food and clothing, let us be content.

1 Timothy 6:7-8

Day 16 - Courage

Dear Lord,

The Bible has given us great examples of courageous people. My children may not have to fight a giant like David did or lead an army like Joshua did. Nevertheless, they will be placed in circumstances where they will need to display courage. Give them courage as they wait on You to make important decisions and choices in their lives. Show me how to equip them with their armor when they may have to fight spiritual battles or spiritual giants. Keep them close to You, Lord, so that You will give them the courage they need. It will take courage to say no when all their friends are saying yes. It will take courage to walk away and separate themselves from things that do not honor You. It will take courage to make some ripples and go against the flow of the world. Help me to speak words of encouragement when they are down in their spirits. Help me to affirm and lift their spirits through Your Word and through examples from the Bible. Keep them strong and mighty in You.

Amen.

A Mother's Prayer for Courage:

_____

_____

_____

_____

_____

_____

_____

_____

_____

_____

_____

_____

_____

_____

Amen.

"I command you—be strong and courageous! Do not be afraid or discouraged. For the LORD your God is with you wherever you go."   Joshua 1:9

Day 17 - Discernment

Dear Lord,

There have been times when I have made decisions without discernment and the consequences have been hard to bear. I know there may also be times in the lives of my children when they may not use discernment, but please let these times be few. Let them learn through mentoring, not by making mistakes, that some decisions have far-reaching consequences. Even when they are grown they may encounter false teachings. I pray that they will have so much of Your Word in their hearts that they will be able to easily discern the truth from a lie. I pray they would seek You for discernment as I also continue to do. King Solomon sought wisdom from You. He knew how vital it was to be wise. Help my children to see how important wisdom and discernment are. Let them be constantly reminded of them. Allow them to use their discernment when making friendships and business agreements, and when choosing a career, a home, and a spouse. Let them be wise beyond their years. I pray that they would fear You, for fearing You is the beginning of wisdom. Help them as they ask You for all things with discernment.

Amen.

A Mother's Prayer for Discernment:

_____

_____

_____

_____

_____

_____

_____

_____

_____

_____

_____

_____

_____

_____

Amen.

*Give discernment to me, your servant; then I will understand
your decrees.* Psalm 119:125

Day 18 - Perseverance

Dear Lord,

There have been times when I have been hard on myself. I have thought, What is the use? It's easier just to quit. I pray I would never have a quitter's spirit. Even if I don't come out in first place, may I never give up. It is the same for my children. Help me not to be so hard on them. I would never want to cause them to want to throw in the towel. Soon enough, my children will go through their teenage years, when their spirits will be vulnerable and when their bodies will be changing in every direction and their emotions flying high. Just as Paul knew what the ultimate goal was, I pray that they would finish their race and never look back or give up. I know that enduring all of this to the end will save them. I ask You to allow perseverance to develop their character through trials in their lives and not to destroy them. I pray and ask that their troubles may be few and that the ones they do endure would not be in vain. Enable me to be their cheerleader. Help me to stand on the sidelines and cheer them on. I know that perseverance through You will give them the crown of life.

Amen.

A Mother's Prayer for Perseverance:

_____

_____

_____

_____

_____

_____

_____

_____

_____

_____

_____

_____

_____

_____

_____

_____

Amen.

We can rejoice, too, when we run into problems and trials, for we know that they are good for us—they help us learn to endure. And endurance develops strength of character in us, and character strengthens our confident expectation of salvation. Romans 5:3-4

Day 19 - Joy

Dear Lord,

I want to always have joy in my life. The choice to maintain my joy is my decision. I can grumble and complain that I have already been called for the eightieth time today and I haven't even made it out of bed, or I can rejoice in the God of my salvation and thank Him that I have strong and healthy children who can call on me. In Your presence is joy. All that You command and call me to do is added joy in my life. I can see the cup half full or half empty. I can choose to be joyful that I have the strength in my body to clean all the little fingerprints off the windows again. I am Your child, and You promise to give me abundant joy. I may not always want to be thankful for the trial, but I can remain thankful to the One who has authority over the trial. Help my children to learn to maintain their joy in all areas of their lives as I first set forth the example. My joy is a direct result of Your Spirit abiding in me. Help my children to stand firm and strong and never lose their joy as they see me joyful before them.

Amen.

A Mother's Prayer for Joy:

_____

_____

_____

_____

_____

_____

_____

_____

_____

_____

_____

_____

_____

_____

Amen.

The commandments of the LORD are right, bringing joy to the heart. The commands of the LORD are clear, giving insight to life.   Psalm 19:8

Day 20 - Faith

Dear Lord,

As we were waiting for our very first chicken eggs to hatch, the hen decided to leave the nest for an undetermined amount of time. We were very close to the day they would hatch, yet found the eggs cold as ice. Everyone we sought advice from told us to throw the eggs away before they started to rot because they would not hatch after being so cold. My children were discouraged and heartbroken over the loss of our first set of eggs. I had decided that if the hen would get back on the nest, despite what everyone was telling us, I would have faith to believe that those eggs would hatch. Every time the children would ask, I would say, "Yes, they are going to hatch." Seven days later, eight chicks had hatched. It was so easy to believe for something so insignificant, so I thought, What about when it is something hard that puts our faith to the test? What if it is a life-or-death situation? When our children are faced with challenges that seem overwhelming, Lord, You provide a shield called faith that is ours for the using. Trials and challenges will test our faith and our children's faith. You will often give us examples to use as teaching tools in our parenting. Just as I had faith for a nest of eggs, how much more faith should I have to believe that You will give my children the faith they need when they need it.

Amen.

A Mother's Prayer for Faith:

_____

_____

_____

_____

_____

_____

_____

_____

_____

_____

_____

_____

_____

_____

Amen.

In every battle you will need faith as your shield to stop the fiery arrows aiming at you by Satan.   Ephesians 6:16

Day 21 - Forgiveness

Dear Lord,

Seventy times seven. That is a lot, Lord. You knew what You were talking about when You said it. Sometimes the offense is so big in my life that it is hard for me to want to forgive. Forgiveness is nothing I can do on my own, but it is an act of my will to choose to do it. There have been times when my children have emotionally wounded me on purpose. It hurt so much. I know You understand. As You hung on the cross for my sins, You forgave the ones who were persecuting You. Even with that head knowledge, why is it still hard to forgive? I cannot do it on my own; I need You. Allow my children to see this need in me. Help me to quickly forgive them when they apologize; this way I too will be forgiven when I offend or hurt someone. Your forgiveness in our lives keeps us clean. I want my children always to be clean before You. Help me to recognize when I sin and let me immediately ask for forgiveness. Teach my children through my example this same quality. Your Spirit in me cleanses me from sin. Thank You for dying for me and for my children. Thank You for providing the way for us to be forgiven.

Amen.

A Mother's Prayer for Forgiveness:

_____

_____

_____

_____

_____

_____

_____

_____

_____

_____

_____

_____

_____

_____

Amen.

*Forgive us our sins, just as we have forgiven those who have
sinned against us.* Matthew 6:12

Day 22 - Self-control

Dear Lord,

I've watched babies interact with one another and it is quite amusing. It is nothing for a baby to reach out and grab a toy from another child, even if it doesn't belong to him, and take possession of it. Babies tend to have no control over their emotions or reactions. This is because they are babies. There are times when I lose my cool and react out of emotion and I am completely out of control. The fruit of self-control is a gift that You have already given to me, and at times I do not use it wisely. I allow my emotions to guide my decisions and I may say or do something that is unacceptable. These are the times when I know I have to be the adult and not behave like a baby. It isn't easy to always be calm, cool, and collected. I want to strive for self-control in my life. I see so many of our youth today out of control. I want to instill in my children today, right where they are, the gift and fruit of self-control. Acting out of emotion is a choice. I want them to always choose self-control in their lives. I want them to be alert to others around them and not react as the world does. Teach us to pray for self-control so that we can continue to live for You. I know that You are the way to self-control. And because I know You, it is attainable not only in my life but also for my children.

Amen.

A Mother's Prayer for Self-control:

_____

_____

_____

_____

_____

_____

_____

_____

_____

_____

_____

_____

_____

_____

Amen.

We are instructed to turn from godless living and sinful pleasures. We should live in this evil world with self-control, right conduct, and devotion to God.			Titus 2:12

Day 23 - Appearance

Dear Lord,

Usually the very first thing we notice about individuals is their outward appearance. At times, we even make judgments against them without allowing any opportunity to get to know who they are. I want my appearance to reflect You. Help me to accept that You look at the heart and the inside person and not at what is on the outside. I know that outward beauty will fade away. Help me never to be vain or to make my children feel so conscious of their appearance that they focus more on the outward than on the inward person. Some of the most beautiful people in this world may have hidden ugliness in their hearts. At the same time, let me also teach my children to value and respect themselves by developing good hygiene habits and by striving to look nice and presentable to please You first and above all. I pray that they would seek first to be attractive on the inside. Help them to understand that true beauty will come from their heart attitude and their actions. Help me to continue to teach them that what is on the inside is what counts the most with You.

Amen.

A Mother's Prayer for Appearance:

_____

_____

_____

_____

_____

_____

_____

_____

_____

_____

_____

_____

_____

_____

Amen.

But the LORD said to Samuel, "Don't judge by his appearance or height, for I have rejected him. The LORD doesn't make decisions the way you do. People judge by outward appearance, but the LORD looks at a person's thoughts and intentions."

1 Samuel 16:7

Day 24 - Character

Dear Lord,

"Character counts" is a cliché we encounter often in our schools and many other places. Character does indeed count. It is something that is important to You. It is also something very important to me. I want to be known positively for my character. I also want my children to value character and strive towards godly character. I know that character is at times developed through the difficulties that we face in everyday life. You are the model; You are the example that has been placed before us of what character looks like. I want my children to be strong assets to Your Kingdom. I know that as their character is built, they will be equipped for anything that this world may offer. Help my children to be aware that their character is rooted in the revelation that they are Your craftsmanship, fashioned after You. I want every word I speak and everything I do, to be a reflection of Your character in me. Allow all of my actions to build up my children's character, not tear it down.

Amen.

A Mother's Prayer for Character:

_____

_____

_____

_____

_____

_____

_____

_____

_____

_____

_____

_____

_____

_____

Amen.

For when your faith is tested, your endurance has a chance to grow. So let it grow, for when your endurance is fully developed, you will be strong in character and ready for anything.   James 1:3-4

Day 25 - Rebellion

Dear Lord,

Why is it that one of the first words my children learned was no? I think about Your servants Mary and Samuel. When You called them to something, yes was their reply. They may not have understood it, but, they were willing nevertheless. I know that the spirit is willing but the flesh is weak. This is true in my life; therefore, I know it is the same for my children. I know that You consider rebellion to be sin. Help my children to consider the consequences of their potential rebellion and then choose not to rebel. I see so many children in this day who rule the parent and the home, instead of the parent being the one in charge. Help me to stand firm and to stand my ground. Help me to be consistent and to honor my word. I pray that the times my children would rebel would be minimal. Help me to train them in Your ways and with the fruit of the Spirit, so that when the temptation to rebel may come, they will demonstrate self-control and overcome the temptation. Help me to determine true rebellion versus childish behaviors so that I am not condemning them for everything they do. While I am carving out the sculpture of my children, help me to tap gently so as not to crush them.

Amen.

A Mother's Prayer for Rebellion:

_____

_____

_____

_____

_____

_____

_____

_____

_____

_____

_____

_____

_____

_____

_____

_____

Amen.

For there are many who rebel against right teaching; they engage in useless talk and deceive people.   Titus 1:10

Day 26 - Anger

Dear Lord,

Anger is a choice. Before I came to this understanding I would usually try to blame some person or some thing for my angriness. The more You have worked in my life, the more I have realized that anger is a choice. If I get angry, it is because I have chosen to be angry. There are a lot of reactions and emotions that I could choose other than being angry. For instance, when I tell my children to make their beds and get dressed for the day and then after an ample of amount of time I check on their progress and find that they are lying on their bed reading a book or something else other than what I have told them, I could easily be angry. I could be angry because of their laziness or I could be angry because I work so hard in the home and when I ask for something to be done, I expect to be listened to and my request to be honored. I can also choose to remain in control of the situation, be the parent, and offer them a choice. They can either obey what I have asked or suffer the consequences of their disobedience. It would be so easy for me to fly off the handle and become angry. I never want anger to be one of the choices of emotions for my life. I know that the only thing anger will teach my children is how to be angry themselves. Your Word tells us not to dwell with angry people. Continue to work in me so that anger is not a part of who I am.

Amen.

A Mother's Prayer for Anger:

_____

_____

_____

_____

_____

_____

_____

_____

_____

_____

_____

_____

_____

_____

_____

Amen.

A gentle answer turns away wrath, but harsh words stir up anger.   Proverbs 15:1

Day 27 - Thankfulness

Dear Lord,

So many times I have come to You with my needs. There have been times when I have prayed and prayed over a situation, specifically needing You to intervene, and when You did, how often I forgot to thank You for working it out. When they are young, saying thank you is one of the first manners we teach our children. I would always try to teach my children to immediately say thank you when they receive a gift. On more than one occasion I would have to nudge them or remind them. These days, people seldom thank anyone for anything. We live in a world where we believe we are owed something. I never want my children to get to a place where they neglect to be thankful to You. Not just for what they can see, not just for what is in Your hand, but to be thankful from their hearts for what You have done for them. Help me never to forget to be thankful for the many blessings, mercy, goodness, and grace that You provide. Help us to tell others what You have done for us. I pray that not only would we speak words of thankfulness to You but also that we would sing praises of thanksgiving to You. I pray that my children's lives would always overflow with thankfulness.

Amen.

A Mother's Prayer for Thankfulness:

_____

_____

_____

_____

_____

_____

_____

_____

_____

_____

_____

_____

_____

_____

_____

Amen.

And you will always give thanks for everything to God the Father in the name of our Lord Jesus Christ.

Ephesians 5:20

Day 28 - Grace

Dear Lord,

Several years ago, I taught my children that when they make a mistake and lose a privilege, one of the best ways to earn it back is to truly ask for forgiveness and then ask for grace to be shown. They have learned this technique very well. My discernment steps in to help me determine if it is genuine or if they just want the privilege back. The dictionary's definition of grace is the capacity to tolerate, accommodate, or forgive people. God's definition of grace is the condition of being free from sin through Jesus Christ after repentance. When my children have been very disobedient and have really gone against my authority, even after they truly repent and ask forgiveness and then ask for grace to be shown, I still don't want to show them grace. My flesh roars up inside of me because I want them to pay for their actions. I am so thankful that You, heavenly Father, do not behave in such a way. Although my flesh wants to say no, when my children ask for grace, I have to show it to them. I know that I have been set free by Your grace. I do not deserve it. I know there is nothing I could ever do to earn it. It is a gift. You gave me a gift and I opened it. I know that Your grace is always sufficient. Help me to continue to show grace in all situations and circumstances, especially to my children.

Amen.

A Mother's Prayer for Grace:

_____

_____

_____

_____

_____

_____

_____

_____

_____

_____

_____

_____

_____

_____

Amen.

So let us come boldly to the throne of our gracious God.
There we will receive his mercy, and we will find grace to
help us when we need it. Hebrews 4:16

Day 29 - Humility

Dear Lord,

There have been so many times in my life when I have been given the opportunity to be humble. When I was in high school, there was a very pretty and popular young lady everyone liked and wanted to be close to. She seldom picked any new friends. Another girl complimented her for the pants she was wearing by letting her know how nice they were, to which she replied, "I know." Help my children never to be so self-absorbed that they forget true humility. To be humble is to always remember to be modest and respectful. I would also ask You to work in them so that they show true humility to all people. I had to remind my son when he received a perfect straight A report card that it was Your wisdom and strength in him, not anything he did on his own. At times we all, including myself, become overwhelmed with how great we are and we forget to humble ourselves before You, Lord. It is only as You are in us that we are truly great. I pray that I would always think of others before myself. I know that when my children serve others, they will learn to be humble. Help my children never to be boastful or arrogant, but always to have a teachable and loving spirit. I ask for opportunities for my children to display true humility.

Amen.

A Mother's Prayer for Humility:

_____

_____

_____

_____

_____

_____

_____

_____

_____

_____

_____

_____

_____

_____

_____

Amen.

Humble yourselves under the mighty power of God, and in his good time he will honor you.   1 Peter 5:6

Day 30 - Jealousy

Dear Lord,

You know my household. You already knew the challenges I would face in raising the children You have given me. I also know that You knew what You were doing and that You did not make a mistake. I know that You put the right children with the right parent at the right time. Having twins has made the battle with jealousy very much a struggle for me. I know it is a struggle for my children at times too. It is so easy to become jealous over what seems to be unimportant. Please help me not to struggle so much trying to keep all things fair. I have learned that counting out the M & M's for a treat is a very important detail. I have also learned to make sure not only that the foods on the plate aren't touching each other but also that the portions are the same. Those things are simple to do. There will be other times in my life and in the lives of my children that may be painful. If one of my children is honored in a certain area, as a mom it is in me to want the other children to receive the same recognition. Help me to realize how unrealistic and unfair this is. Help me to assure my children that they are all very special and that they each have different gifts and talents that God wants them to use. Just because one may receive an award in math and another receives one in art, there is no reason to be jealous. Help me to teach them to rejoice for one another, knowing that they will excel in different areas.

Amen.

A Mother's Prayer for Jealousy:

_____
_____
_____
_____
_____
_____
_____
_____
_____
_____
_____
_____
_____
_____
_____

Amen.

Love is patient and kind. Love is not jealous or boastful or proud. 1 Corinthians 13:4-5